John Wordsworth

On the Rite of Consecration of Churches

Especially in the Church of England

John Wordsworth

On the Rite of Consecration of Churches
Especially in the Church of England

ISBN/EAN: 9783744708784

Printed in Europe, USA, Canada, Australia, Japan

Cover: Foto ©Lupo / pixelio.de

More available books at **www.hansebooks.com**

𝕿𝖍𝖊 𝕮𝖍𝖚𝖗𝖈𝖍 𝕳𝖎𝖘𝖙𝖔𝖗𝖎𝖈𝖆𝖑 𝕾𝖔𝖈𝖎𝖊𝖙𝖞.

President:—THE RIGHT REVEREND M. CREIGHTON, D.D.,
LORD BISHOP OF LONDON.

Chairman:—THE REVEREND W. E. COLLINS,
PROFESSOR OF ECCLESIASTICAL HISTORY
AT KING'S COLLEGE, LONDON.

LII.

On the Rite of Consecration of Churches,

ESPECIALLY IN THE CHURCH OF ENGLAND.

𝕬 𝕷𝖊𝖈𝖙𝖚𝖗𝖊

BY

JOHN WORDSWORTH,

BISHOP OF SALISBURY.

*TOGETHER WITH THE FORM OF PRAYER AND
ORDER OF CEREMONIES IN USE IN THE
DIOCESE OF SALISBURY.*

PUBLISHED UNDER THE DIRECTION OF THE TRACT COMMITTEE.

LONDON:
SOCIETY FOR PROMOTING CHRISTIAN KNOWLEDGE.
NORTHUMBERLAND AVENUE, W.C.; 43, QUEEN VICTORIA STREET, E

BRIGHTON: 129, NORTH STREET.
NEW YORK: E. & J. B. YOUNG & CO.
1899.

CONTENTS.

—⧎—

This Lecture was delivered at the Fourth Annual Meeting of the Church Historical Society, held at Sion College, on Thursday, 8 December, 1898.

ON THE RITE OF
CONSECRATION OF CHURCHES,

ESPECIALLY IN THE CHURCH OF ENGLAND.

———

Introduction.

My interest in the subject to which I have the privilege to call the attention of the Church Historical Society is naturally in great measure one of a practical character. Being called as a Bishop to consecrate Churches, some of them of considerable importance, and finding myself without authoritative direction as to the rite to be followed, I have almost inevitably had to consider what history might suggest on the subject. Two occasions especially have stimulated this inquiry, the consecration of Marlborough College Chapel, on Michaelmas Day, 1886, and that of the Collegiate Church of St. George at Jerusalem, on St. Luke's Day, 1898, from which I have recently returned. Both opportunities have been used by me for the Revision of the current *Form and Order* which has come down to us from the beginning of the last century, the first revision for general Diocesan use being published in 1887, the second in the present year (1898). The latter, I may remark, was used for the first time a few weeks before my journey to Jerusalem, at the consecration of the beautiful new Church built by Viscount Portman at his Dorset home in the parish of Bryanston. Our Sarum form differs from all others that I have as yet seen in containing certain appropriate music, which I owe to the kindness of Precentor Carpenter and Mr. W. S. Bambridge, organist of Marlborough College, for which part of it was composed in 1886. In these revisions I have had the assistance of able liturgists, amongst whom I may especially name Dr. W. Bright, of Christ Church, Oxford, Mr. Brightman, of the Pusey House, Mr. Charles Druitt, Vicar of Whitchurch Canonicorum, and my brother, Christopher Wordsworth, now Rector of S. Peter's, Marlborough. The final responsibility, however, has rested solely with myself.

It is mainly with the view of setting before you the principles on which this revision seems to me to rest, and of encouraging a like revision in other Dioceses (which may some day, I hope, lead to the adoption of a worthy and truly characteristic rite by the Church of England as a body) that I have gladly accepted the offer made to me through your Chairman. He has, I may remark, himself studied the subject, and given me assistance in preparing this lecture by communicating to me the contents of the important collection of consecration forms at Lambeth.

I. It is not easy to determine what were the first rites and ceremonies in use when buildings for Christian worship were set apart for the service of God. Nor even when we come to the important historical dedications of the reign of Constantine the Great, in the early part of the fourth century, are we able to discern much light in the vague and inflated descriptions of Eusebius. The probability seems to be that the only essentials were a transference of previous ownership on the part of the Founder, and an acceptance of the trust by the Bishop of the Diocese on behalf of the Church, followed by a *solemn celebration of the Holy Eucharist.* The part played by the Founder or Builder would in accordance with Jewish and heathen precedent be a considerable one; and Christian custom, acting in accordance with the principles of Roman law, would prescribe the dedication by solemn and ceremonial use. The "usurpatio juris" of the Christian Society in its new home could hardly be otherwise exemplified than by the Sacrament in which believers, gathered under the presidency of their chief pastor, came together to meet their Lord in His new house, to plead His sacrifice and to feast upon it. Of course, the mere celebration of Christian mysteries in a place could not consecrate it, as Synesius remarks in a letter (Ep. 67) quoted by Bingham; nor could a consecration take place except with the full consent, formally expressed, of the previous owner of the site and building. Hence we find S. Athanasius apologizing at length to the Emperor Constantius for using a church founded by him, before its consecration, owing to the press of worshippers, and expressing a hope that he would come and assist at the ceremony of its dedication (*Apologia ad Constantium*, 14–18, an important passage). But, supposing the necessary conditions, it would seem that the solemn Eucharist was the only essential ceremony. It is worth noting in this connexion that the words κυριακόν and "Dominicum" are used both in Greek and Latin for the Lord's House or Temple and the Lord's Supper or Sacrifice [1]. The Eucharist is in fact the most distinctly Christian rite, that which proves a Church to be a Church. The Baptistery or Font may be and often is outside; but the holy Table can be no where but in the most prominent place of the Sanctuary.

I therefore agree in this point with that learned French professor, the Abbé Duchesne, whom I am glad to be able to count as a friend, who in his well-known book on the "origins of Christian worship" expresses himself to the following effect:—Towards the middle of the sixth century when Pope Vigilius wrote to Profuturus of Braga A.D. 538 "the Church of Rome had no ritual for the dedication of Churches. A Church was dedicated merely by the fact that Mass had been solemnly celebrated in it" (*Origines du culte Chrétien*, p. 389, 1889). A reminiscence of this ancient principle is found surely in the provision of Canon Law, attributed, no doubt falsely, to two different early popes, but probably embodying ancient tradition:—"Omnes basilicae cum missa debent semper consecrari." "All basilicas (apparently churches of all kinds) must always be consecrated with the celebration of a mass" (see Burchardus, iii. *decret.* 27, 21, as from Evaristus A.D. 96 and Gratian *de consecr.* dist. 1, c. 3, as from Hyginus A.D. 138). Of similar effect is the prohibition, adopted by various authorities, and sometimes ascribed to Pope Sylvester (A.D. 324) "Nullus Presbyter missas celebrare praesumat nisi in sacratis ab episcopo locis [2]."

The ascription of these canons to early popes is mere guess-work, or worse; but they seem to represent the expressed principles of the Church as early as the ninth century, and probably go back in substance to a remote antiquity.

---

[1] See Suicer s. v. κυριακόν for instances of both. S. Athanasius, writing to Constantius, speaks of his new Church at Alexandria, and takes for granted that he would wish the people to pray for him, ἐν τῷ ἐπωνύμῳ σου τόπῳ ὃν ἤδη, μᾶλλον δὲ καὶ ἅμα τῷ θεμελίῳ, κυριακὸν πάντες ὀνομάζουσιν. For "Dominicum" in both senses see S. Cyprian, *de op. et eleem.* 15, cp. Ep. 63, 16.

[2] Gratian, l. c. cap. 15; cp. cap. 12.

Whatever be the origin of these rules, there is no doubt that when Bishops of the Church of England began again to consecrate churches in the reign of King James I, they generally accepted the pre-reformation tradition on this point by making a celebration of Holy Communion an integral part of the rite. We find it in the forms used by Bishop Barlow of Lincoln in 1610, Bishop Andrewes in 1620, Bishop George Monteigne of London in 1622, Bishop William Laud of London on several occasions, 1630–1632, Bishop White of Ely at Peterhouse, 1632, Bishop Theophilus Field of Hereford at Abbey Dore in 1634, Archbishop Neile of York at Leeds, 1634, Bishop Cosin of Durham after the Restoration 1665, and the Irish form of 1666 onwards. It is clearly implied in the forms which were drawn up but left unfinished by Convocation in 1712 and 1715, and which, of course, never received Royal Assent, but have more currency than any others. The only seeming exceptions known to me in the seventeenth century are two rather obscure cases of consecrations by Bishop King of London and Bishop Moreton of Chester in 1615 and 1616, very shortly described by Collier (*Hist.* ii. 709). He gives only the Consecration prayer, and says: "After this a Psalm was sung and the Bishop dismissed the Congregation with his blessing." The prayer might come at the end of a celebration, or, what is still more probable, the Bishop dismissed the mass of the people with an intermediate blessing, and then went on with the communion for those who remained. Bishop King's register contains notes of the consecrations of St. Olave's, Silver Street, in 1610 and of the Chapel of Lord Bridgwater in Willoughby House in 1620, but (according to Dr. J. Wickham Legg, who has kindly made the search for me) no liturgical forms are given. There is a form of consecrating St. Sepulchre's Churchyard in 1612.

As regards opinion on the point of the celebration of the Eucharist the only one known to me is that of Bishop Gibson in his *Codex* (p. 189), who after quoting the maxim of the Canon Law: "Omnes basilicae cum missa debent semper consecrari," adds: "The gloss makes a doubt whether this is not *de substantia Consecrationis*: but be that as it will, it is certainly very decent." Had he inquired a little more deeply into the matter he could perhaps have spoken even more strongly. His own form, used in 1729 at Christ Church, in the Parish of St. Dunstan, Stepney, may be seen, with a number of others, in Oughton's *Ordo Judiciorum*

(2 p. 256 foll.), which shows that he followed the form of 1715 in this point. See also his *Codex*, ii. 1459-62.

I have examined a number of the Registers of my predecessors in the Diocese of Salisbury, and find the same usage on the point in question, though I cannot claim to have exhausted every instance. Nor can I venture to state when it became a matter of question whether the administration of the Lord's Supper should take place or not. But, I think, I may say with confidence that when the change was made in any diocese it was first made in the form of the half measure of stopping after the sermon or after the prayer for the Church. The special Collect, Epistle, and Gospel were always used. This process is illustrated by the form of Consecration adopted by the Church of the United States of America, the first branch of our communion to make such a form authoritative, which it did in 1799. The form is nearly that of 1715, but with some slight alterations, and the addition of a post-communion collect from the form of 1712. But it treats the celebration as uncertain : *The Sermon being ended the Bishop shall proceed in the service for the Communion, if it is to be administered at that time.* It is interesting, however, to note that the rubrics dealing with this contingency have been removed at the last revision of the American Prayer Book in 1886, and, as the service now stands, the Communion is taken for granted. The opening rubric simply is : *The Bishop shall then proceed to the Communion service,* and at the end, *For the last collect immediately before the final Blessing, the Bishop shall say this Prayer :* Blessed be Thy Name, &c.

The procedure of the modern Irish Church is even more explicit. The rubric is as follows :—*Communion service. The Bishop shall read the service, and the Holy Communion shall be administered,* and then follow special Collect, Epistle, and Gospel, and two final or post-communion Collects.

The uncertainty with regard to the celebration is reflected in the reprint of the current Form, edited by the much-respected Archdeacon of Oxford, Rev. C. C. Clerke, in 1833, and often reprinted afterwards, in the following rubric : *The sermon being ended, if there be no Communion, the Prayer for the Church militant shall be read.* It was, however, the practice of Bishop Samuel Wilberforce to have the celebration, as I learn from his son, the present Bishop of Chichester ; and it is prescribed in the Diocesan *Form* of 1864.

It was not strange that in the early part of this century, and in quarters where ritual matters were not much attended to, there should have been sometimes a resort to this half-measure; but it is, I think, somewhat surprising to find that in some cases at the close of this nineteenth century the celebration is wholly dropped, or is made a prelude to the service of consecration by being taken at an early hour. The best motive for this practice is one which I know has weighed with some of my brethren, namely, the desire to have as large a congregation as possible at an evening service. I venture to think that this would be quite admissible provided that the celebration did not precede but followed the consecration at an early hour the next morning. This in fact would have something primitive about it, and would be in harmony with the usage of the Greek Church, especially if the consecration were continued by vigils, carried on by relays of worshippers through the night. The Bishop, however, who consecrated the Church should certainly be the celebrant, the first celebrant, in the new Church next morning. If there is any principle worth fighting for in an Episcopal Church it is that of Diocesan Unity; and this cannot be upheld with distinctness unless the Bishop visibly asserts, on so important an occasion in the life of a parish as the consecration of a new church, that he is the ordinary minister of its spiritual life, and not merely a distant functionary called in to perform duties which the incumbent cannot do. I make this clear to all incumbents at their Institution by using the formula "Accipe curam meam ac tuam"; but that act of Institution is not always performed before their people. What is needed is to show to them that each Church is the Church of the Bishop, though for the sake of convenience, and indeed out of physical necessity, he is obliged to delegate his daily duties to it to a presbyter under certain canonical rules and safeguards, and in subservience to a system which, of course, practically binds him not to interfere too often or too curiously with the ordinary management of the Church services.

II. As regards the ancient peculiar rites of consecration they may be described as extensions of two conceptions:—(1) a formal taking over the place in the name of our Lord Jesus Christ, and a dedicating of it to Him with rites in a great measure parallel to those by which the living Christian is dedicated in baptism and confirmation; (2) a translation and burial of relics of martyrs, by which the altar becomes the covering of a tomb.

Under the first head may be grouped solemn processions, exor-

cisms, lustrations, washings, cuttings or paintings of crosses, anoint-
ings with various mixtures, especially of chrism, burning of many
lights, incense and the like. These, though much more elaborate in
the west than the east, are in a degree common to both. But
in some later western sacramentaries appears a peculiar rite, which
has no position in Greek service-books, which certainly was not
ancient Roman, and may be Milanese, Gallican, Celtic, or Spanish,
viz. the drawing of a cross formed by the letters of an alphabet
twice repeated on the floor of the nave. It is found, for example,
in the ninth century Milan Pontifical, in the Egbert, Jumièges, and
Dunstan Pontificals (not Leofric A), and in the old Irish use
described in the *Spotted Book* (*Leabhar Breac*, ed. Rev. T. Olden,
S. Paul's Ecclesi. Soc. iv. 102), which gives a rite probably in use as
late as the first half of the twelfth century and probably derived
from ancient times. I will speak first of this latter ceremony,
which occurs comparatively early in the order, and is, in my
opinion, really antecedent to the whole service. In trying to solve
the mystery which attaches to it the Abbé Duchesne quotes an
interesting article by the great Roman archæologist, Commendatore
G. B. de Rossi, contained in his *Bullettino di Archeologia Cristiana*
for 1881, pp. 140–195, which I have examined. De Rossi connects
the alphabetic cross with the cross drawn by the Roman augurs in
laying out a templum, and by the agrimensores in measuring land
for a colony, &c. The Bishop draws with the point of his pastoral
staff a St. Andrew's cross, connecting the four angles of the
body of the church, on ashes or sand previously spread upon the
floor, consisting of the Greek Alphabet along one line and then
the Latin Alphabet along the other. This is the present rite ;
though from some early Sacramentaries it would seem that the
Latin alphabet was twice written. Mention is also made of the
Hebrew alphabet as being occasionally used (in Menard's notes to
the Gregorian Sacramentary). The difficulty, however, of directly
connecting this procedure with the surveyor's art, from which De
Rossi derives it, is very considerable. The cross made by them
was one of four right angles, and was composed of two lines
forming the minor and the major axis of the templum, one the
" cardo maximus " running north and south, the other the " decumanus limes" running east and west—or perhaps more correctly
west to east. If, therefore, the rite had been directly borrowed
from the agrimensores the form of it would not have been a

St. Andrew's cross uniting the four corners, but a true cross, like the St. George's cross on our flags, cutting the four sides into equal portions. I have not carefully studied the orientation of churches, but I imagine it is pretty certain that it followed the orientation of heathen temples, whether a heathen temple were converted into a church, like the Temple of Jupiter, at Baalbek, or a new church were built like the Basilica of Constantine at Jerusalem and the Vatican at Rome. Early basilicas mostly had the altar at the west end: see G. G. Scott, *History of E. Ch. Architecture*, p. 14 foll. But all ran on the same lines.

It is true that, as De Rossi observes, the alphabet plays a great part in the writings of the agrimensores (libri gromatici). He mentions one use of it, the "casae litterarum," which, with all deference, I hardly think that he quite understands. He might also have mentioned two others. The surveyors used the alphabet, just as Euclid did, to help them to identify lines and angles in their plans. They used it also as a series of symbols for certain measures of length, so many feet or "podismi." The "casae litterarum," however, in which both the Latin and Greek alphabets were used, were symbols referring to certain typical plans, one of an Italian, the other of a foreign settlement. Each letter represented a particular farm or spot on the map with certain peculiarities attaching to it, and the pupils were expected to know by heart what each of these letters signified. I do not, however, find that these letters were attached to the cardo and decumanus of the surveyors, indeed they seem to have been scattered all about the plans.

While, therefore, it is possible that there may be some relation between the laying out of a heathen temple and the "abecedarium," as it is technically called, in the dedication of a church, the latter can hardly have been directly derived from the former. The peculiar Christian rite may have been adopted from a vague memory of a method of which the true tradition was lost. De Rossi, however, suggests a second explanation, which to myself appears more full of meaning, viz. that the St. Andrew's cross, or Chi, is the initial of the name of Christ in Greek, as also in Latin MSS, which write the name in three letters, $\overline{XPS}$. To me the alphabet seems to be also another symbol of Christ as the word of God, not only Alpha and Omega, but all that lies between, every element, in fact, of human speech.

If this be so it is a very natural part of a service, the main thought of which is to take the place to be consecrated into the keeping of a new Master. To write His name upon it would be a very fitting mark of His ownership. I conjecture also that the ceremony belonged to the laying out of the first sketch or foundation of the building rather than to the actual consecration, and that (as usual), in process of time, diverse ceremonies were heaped together without much regard to their congruity. It would answer to the σταυροπήγιον of the Greeks and to the laying of a foundation stone among ourselves. This, of course, would agree quite as well with De Rossi's theory as with that which I think more probable. In fact, he notices in confirmation of this suggestion, that antiphons having reference to Christ as a foundation were sung at the same time (p. 143). I presume this refers to the antiphon "Fundamentum aliud nemo potest ponere praeter illud denique quod positum est a Christo Domino," followed by the psalm "Fundamenta eius," which I find in Jumièges, Dunstan, De Bernham, and elsewhere.

If, therefore, we were inclined to adopt this alphabet ceremony in any form among ourselves, it should be at the laying of the foundation stone of the church, rather than at its dedication. I may remark, in passing, that the introduction of ashes on which to write looks very like a later artifice to. enable the Bishop to do something which at first he would have been able to do without difficulty. Speaking generally, the St. Andrew's cross traced on the bare earth or sand would be the simplest way possible of giving the dimensions of the nave and taking possession of the whole space to be consecrated in the name of Christ. The surveyor's cross would require something in the nature of a rule and compasses to complete the outline exactly: but the St. Andrew's cross, given the four corners, would only need to have them joined by a piece of cord or twine. In practice, I suppose, the four corners would be represented by angle stones. I can conceive it a very reasonable part of the ceremony of the foundation of a church, that these four stones should bear the Alpha and Omega and the A and Z of the Greek and Latin alphabets in their proper respective positions, and that the Bishop with his staff should trace a Chi cross connecting them. Or, if the principle were adopted, the first and last letters of the Hebrew and Greek alphabets respectively might be inscribed on the stones in order to symbolize the union of the Jewish and Gentile Churches. It is not absolutely certain whether the drawing began from the eastern or the western part of the nave. The evidence, however, of the oldest books I have had access to is in favour of beginning at the east. This is the usage described in the Gregorian Sacramentary, the *Spotted Book* and the Egbert, Jumièges, Dunstan, Milan, De Bernham, and so-called York *Pontificals.*

Nearly all bid us to begin from the "left-hand eastern corner." The *Spotted Book* says more explicitly: "The first alphabet begins from the south-east angle and is finished at the north-west angle. The second alphabet begins at the north-east angle and is finished at the south-west angle, so that the two O's meet in the middle of the floor." Nothing, I may remark, is here said as to sprinkling sand or ashes. Of course, "left" and "right" are ambiguous terms, as we know is the case in regard to the parts of the altar, and I think that all these uses may be intended to commence at the south-east. On the other hand the modern Roman Pontifical bids the Bishop begin from the corner on his left as he enters, which in a church entered by a west door would, of course, be the north-west. This would, however, so far agree with the *Spotted Book* as to make the first alphabet traced by the diagonal running north-west and south-east. I venture, therefore, to suggest the following arrangement of angle stones, whether the full alphabet be traced or not.

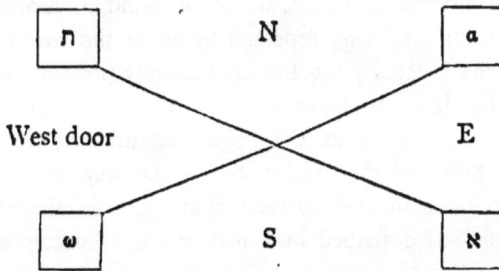

III. Besides this "Abecedarium" the main group of ceremonies, i. e: those really proper to consecration, contains some that simply signify taking possession, especially the processional circuit, and others more explicitly dedicatory, analogous to baptism and confirmation, including those for the expulsion of evil spirits. The procession taking possession of the church-site has precedents in the Old Testament, as well as in the innocent ceremonial of heathen religion. It seems, indeed, to be well worthy of being revived among us, and we have, therefore, restored it in our Diocesan form, though restricting it to one instead of three circuits. We have naturally omitted the ceremonies of lustration and purifi-

cation which imply that the place has previously been the abode of
evil spirits, and have changed a preliminary Latin collect, which
suggested it, for a simpler Greek one which prays that the holy
angels may enter as fellow servants in our worship. The driving
out of evil spirits might not be out of place when a heathen temple
was taken over for God's service, as was frequently the case in early
days. But it does not seem appropriate in a country long
Christian, and a new building made of God's good creatures of
wood, stone, iron, and the rest. We have, however, restored the
simple and expressive ceremony of knocking at the door with the
butt of the pastoral staff, with the old antiphon and response, *Lift
up your heads*, &c., after which follows the entrance and the new
symbolic action of taking possession in the delivery of the keys to
the Bishop as representative head of the Christian family which is to
inhabit and use the house. The Bishop then says a triple word of
peace, adapted from the antiphon given in Maskell's copy, which he
calls the Sarum use, and not, as far as I am aware, found in others.
This may be considered as the ceremony in the Anglican rite,
which is analogous to Baptism, in the name of the Blessed Trinity.
We then say the antiphon *Lift up your heads* with Response, and
then the twenty-fourth Psalm, which is found in nearly all ritual
books, the antiphon being repeated by all at the conclusion. On
arriving at the sanctuary the Bishop solemnly presents the keys on
the table that is to be hallowed, with a prayer addressed to our
Lord in His attributes as the beginning and the ending of all
things, the first and the last, who has the key of the house of
David, who openeth and no man shutteth, who shutteth and no
man openeth—as described in Isaiah and the Apocalypse—asking
that the Church now opened for His service may ever be filled with
His presence and remain a refuge for His faithful people.

Then follows the hymn, Veni Creator, which may be considered
the Anglican analogue to the ceremonies borrowed from the rite of
confirmation in the western service-books.

Then I have recently introduced two features borrowed from the
Greek Euchologion, viz. the Litany, or Ectene, and a special long
consecration prayer, which latter appears to me more beautiful and
suitable than any Latin prayer or any already in use in our own
current forms. I draw attention to these features because they
should be subject to criticism if any criticism is to be made, either
to-day or on a future occasion. The Litany is that generally

familiar, beginning " Stretch out thy hand upon us O Lord and save us, pity us, raise us up, and defend us," with the response, " O Lord have mercy," and containing special reference to the work in hand and the name to be given to the Church. The long prayer refers to God's instructions to Moses, Bezaleel, Solomon, and the Apostles, and contains petitions for those who perform the work of consecration, describing the offices to be performed in the building, and its general character as "a haven for the tempest-tossed, a place of healing for sufferers, a refuge for the sick, a defence against evil spirits." In this also the name is mentioned.

In the Greek rite the Prayer is said by the Bishop kneeling on a cushion at the doors of the screen, the Litany by the Deacon, with a common Doxology. I have directed that the Litany should be said as an introduction to the Prayer, and that the Bishop should stand.

IV. Then follows the actual consecration of the Church, which may be considered as analogous to the rite of Ordination, as the preliminary part is to the rites of Baptism and Confirmation. In the western rituals this centres specially upon the altar, although there are numerous processions about the church, within and without, scattering water upon the walls and the pavement, and finally a marking of twelve crosses with chrism upon the walls on places indicated, some of which still remain visible in Salisbury Cathedral and elsewhere. It is said that the English use differed from the foreign in having crosses both within and without. The Irish use shows its primitive character in ordering the crosses to be cut with a knife, no doubt on wooden posts, &c. But there is generally in these old forms no definite recognition of the other sacramental rites and devotional uses of the church besides the great Sacrament of the altar [1]. Just, therefore, as the English ordinal for the Priesthood differs from the Roman in its emphasis on *all* the duties of the ministry of the word and sacraments, while the Roman tends to exalt the ministry of the altar into excessive prominence, it is fitting that the Anglican rite of consecration of churches should be of a like broad and yet explicit character.

We owe it mainly to the genius and liturgical instinct of Bishop Andrewes that this conception already exists in services current among us. He seems to have been the first among us to introduce

---

[1] The *Benedictio fontis* is mentioned in the Leofric Missal (ed. Warren p. 219 a). This part was written in Loraine, where Leofric himself was trained.

a procession to different spots in the Church connected with different rites. Bishop William Barlow, of Lincoln, indeed, in 1610, had consecrated the font, but no mention seems to be made of his dedicating the holy table or any other object. Bishop Andrewes' practice was much fuller. All that we have done is to follow his leadership, and to make the procession, which he prescribes, to different parts of the Church a little more solemn and particular, adding to it appropriate passages of holy Scripture to be chanted before the prayers said at the respective places. Andrewes' places. are the font, pulpit, reading desk, holy table, place of marriage, and pavement, with reference specially to the dead, who may hereafter be buried under it—possibly a kind of concession to the instinct for communion with the departed, which in some of the pre-reformation services raised the burial of relics into such exaggerated prominence. ,

Laud, in consecrating the Church of Stanmore Magna, followed the same order in this particular, except that he seems to have omitted the blessing of the reading desk (Harington, p. 198). Field, of Hereford, follows Bishop Andrewes exactly in this matter, and also makes provision [1] (as Andrewes seems to have done) for the actual performance of the ceremonies of baptism, marriage, and churching, when desired at the same service. Archbishop Neile (in the same year, 1634) seems also to have been content with Andrewes' practice (Russell's *Abbey Doře*, p. 38). On the other hand, Monteigne's service, as Bishop of London (1622), seems to have been, on the whole, much simpler, and after the type, I presume, of King's, consisting chiefly of one long consecration prayer. As he was almost the immediate predecessor of Laud, it was perhaps natural that the latter's procedure should be more severely criticized.

Bishop Cosin, after the Restoration, has the same idea of a pro-, cession to different places, but his series varies slightly from Andrewes'. It consists of " the Font," " the place where the Lessons are read," " the place where Morning and Evening Prayer is made," " the pulpitt," " the pavement," " the Table of the Lord," thus adding one (the place of Morning and Evening Prayer) and omitting one (viz. the place of Marriage). Another even more interesting form is that printed in several of the Irish Prayer-books from 1666 onwards, and which possibly received some Convocational, as well as

[1] Cp. Harington, 160, *Pergitur in Liturgia*, &c.

B

considerable Archiepiscopal and Episcopal authority. It was re-printed by the Society for Promoting Christian Knowledge in 1893, with a learned introduction from the pen of Bishop William Reeves of Down and Connor. It is long, and has long prayers, apparently original, and probably on account of the quaintness of some of these it may have fallen into disuse. Bishop Reeves, from a detached note, appears finally to have supposed it to be the compilation of Archbishop King of Dublin, but this must be a mistake, as King was born in 1650 and did not become Archbishop till 1688. There are special lessons and prayers to be said at font and pulpit and at the "altar or communion table," as well as a prayer at the offering of the sacred vessels, books, utensils, &c. There are various traces of Greek influence, especially a prayer from the end of St. Clement's Epistle, and a Psalm called "the Anathematism" (from Psalms 79, 83, 129), followed by an "Euphemism" from Psalms 150, 68, 87, 99, 100. Morning Prayer is to be said and Confirmation (if possible) administered, and Communion is to follow.

It is characteristic of the staid and reserved attitude of the religion of the eighteenth century, that prayers answering to the prayers said in different places, are directed to be said by the Bishop "continuing where he is," i.e. without anything of a procession, in the form of 1712. These words were omitted in the last draft of the service of 1715 (which was, as is well known, never completed by Convocation, though generally agreed to), but the rest of the rubric remains, which bids him say them standing up "turning his face toward the congregation," and therefore implies that he is to remain where he is. The prayers then accepted—and continued more or less in use to the present day—add a reference to confirmation and to those who come to return thanks for mercies received. The chief addition of importance that they have received is in the Irish Prayer-book, where to the series is joined a collect for those "who shall be admitted here to any office in the Sacred Ministry" of God's Church. The prayer about returning thanks has also been dropped by the Irish.

Few, I imagine, and perhaps no one here, will doubt that Bishop Andrewes' method of saying such prayers at the appropriate places is much more impressive than the repetition of them in a series. I am certain that our Diocesan Form, first used at Marlborough in 1886, was not the first to set the very obvious example of this return to seventeenth-century usage, but I should be glad of explicit information on the subject [1]. What we may more probably claim as our contribution, is the choice of appropriate passages of Scripture which, as I have said, are sung before each prayer. Our series of places is Font, Chancel Step (for memorials of marriage and confirmation vows), Lectern, Pulpit, Stalls of the Clergy, Choir Seats, Sanctuary Steps, including a blessing of the Lord's Table, of Ornaments and Vessels, and a prayer for communicants. The matter contained in these prayers is partly old, partly new.

Then follow in our form the Antiphons " Christ hath reconciled us unto God in one body by the Cross, having slain the enmity thereby. Surely the Lord is in this place. This is none other than the house of God, and this is the gate of Heaven," and then the final series of short prayers, especially for the worshippers, which come originally also from Andrewes, but are omitted in the Convocation Forms and by the Irish and Americans. Then follow the Antiphons " Behold a ladder set up on the earth," &c. and "Surely the Lord is in this place," &c., and then the sentence of consecration, after which follows the Communion service without Morning Prayer.

The form used in Sarum Diocese has largely influenced that put out by the late Bishop How of Wakefield, which, being printed and sold by the Society for Promoting Christian Knowledge, has obtained a certain currency and influence. I cannot honestly say that I think the result is as satisfactory as it might have been if he had adopted our service as it stood. The Bishop of Winchester has adopted another plan, which is very natural under the circumstances, viz. a reprint, with some modifications, of Bishop Andrewes' form. The most interesting of the other forms known to me are that of Cumbrae, consecrated as a Cathedral by Bishop George Mackarness in 1876, that of Truro Cathedral in 1887, and that now used in the Diocese of Edinburgh.

V. As regards the second conception on which pre-reformation rites of consecration rest, viz. the translation and burial of relics of martyrs, by which the altar becomes a tomb, I may refer you to

[1] The first case actually known to me is that of Cumbrae (1876) which has prayers at Font, Chancel Steps (Confirmation, Marriage, Confession), Altar Steps (Communion, Ordination), Altar. Earlier supposed cases such as St. Ninian's Cathedral, Perth, by Bishop A. P. Forbes in 1850, and St. Barnabas, Pimlico, by Bishop Blomfield, in the same year, are not described with sufficient clearness.

the excellent sketch given by the Abbé Duchesne in his *Origines.*
The Church owes him a debt for showing how these rites grew
from rare occasions of real burials or translations in cemetery
chapels to formalities prescribed for nearly all churches. The
process is clearly part of the exaggerated and unhealthy cultus of
the saints which developed very rapidly in the fourth century, and
which since that time has been hanging like a cloud on the edge
of every church movement in nearly every century, ready to
encumber it and confuse men's minds. Fourth-century Christians
of an older type, with devotional instincts in excess of their
understanding, felt a profound but unbalanced reverence for their
fathers in the faith, whose struggles and victories had led up to
their own assured peace. Christians also of the new type, taken
over in masses from heathenism with very insufficient convictions,
were glad to find a series of minor sacred personages with whose
cultus they could associate the thoughts previously connected with
the local and inferior deities of their old religion. Relic burial
may even have been in some degree a survival of the barbarous
"foundation-sacrifice" of paganism. See *note* p. 26. The strength
of this instinct is seen not only in popular Christianity, but in
popular Judaism and Mahomedanism, where tombs of saints and
patriarchs take to a great extent the place of heathen shrines.

At first, as Duchesne reminds us, the relics were actual bodies
of martyrs, either buried in cemetery chapels, which were rebuilt
in a more splendid form when the Church became dominant,
or translated and deposited in them. Then came the stage of
imitation, when the popularity of such cemetery chapels, and the
abuses connected with them, led active churchmen to wish to
establish other shrines in the cities under better control. Such
a case was that of the Ambrosian Basilica at Milan in 386, when
St. Ambrose opportunely discovered the supposed remains of two
gigantic martyrs, Gervasius and Protasius, who had suffered over
300 years before. His enthusiasm on this occasion gave a great
impetus to the practice. In course of time it became usual to
have relics in all churches, if not actual fragments of bodies, yet
something which had touched or been connected with a saint. It
might be a scrap of a garment or of a covering of his tomb,
a handkerchief bathed in blood, or a phial of oil from the lamp of
his sanctuary. With this all the formalities of a burial service were
gone through just as if it had been a body. Or if even this could

not be obtained, then fragments of the Gospels were solemnly buried, or the consecrated Eucharist. The latter custom was disapproved by Pope Innocent IV (A.D. 1243-1254) and is now out of use. But it was once very common[1].

How far the ceremony of relic burial was an essential or even a common circumstance of the consecration of churches in England has not as yet been fully discussed, though Mr. Dewick and Mr. Olden have made valuable contributions to a study of the question.

No doubt it was the general policy of the Roman Church to promote the custom, and this is evident in the letter of Gregory the Great to Mellitus (Bede, *E. H.* i. 30, Greg. *Ep.* xi. 76, &c.), withdrawing the advice that he had given to Ethelbert to destroy idol temples, and advising Augustine to destroy the idols, sprinkle holy water on the temples, to construct altars, and deposit relics. In agreement with this advice we find Gregory in his *Dialogues* referring to the rededication of an Arian Church at Rome with the relics of St. Sebastian and St. Agatha (*Dial.* iii. 30). It is also the case that in the earliest type of Pontifical we possess, that of Egbert, the use of relics is provided for in the consecration of churches (ed. Greenwell, Surtees Soc. p. 45 foll. 1853).

On the other hand there is negative evidence, extending to the sixteenth century, that the use of actual relics was not insisted upon, and that it was an *Anglican usage* to dispense with them.

The first and, if I am not mistaken, the only canon of the Church of England describing the consecration of a Church runs as follows, as far as the very ungrammatical Latin admits of translation: " Where Churches are built they are to be hallowed by the Bishop of their own Diocese. Let the water be blessed by himself [and] let it be sprinkled, and so let it be finished as it is contained in the Ministerial book. Afterwards let the Eucharist, which is consecrated by the Bishop in the same service, be enclosed in a little box with other relics and preserved in the same Basilica. And, if he is not able to insert other relics, yet this by itself can especially avail, because it is the Body and Blood of our Lord Jesus Christ. Or (seu) we further enjoin to each Bishop that he have painted on the

---

[1] See esp. Scudamore, *Notitia Eucharistica*, ed. 2, 916-9, and the second chapter of the Council of Celchyth or Chelsea, A. D. 816, in Haddan and Stubbs, ii. p. 580, or Wilkins, *Concilia*, i. p. 169, and Lyndwood, *Provinciale* (A. D. 1446), p. 249, note m, Oxon., 1679.

wall of the Oratory or on a board, or even on the altars, to what
saints both of them (nave and chancel?) are dedicated " (Council
of Celchyth, chap. ii). It is no unfair inference from this canon
that the use of relics in England was by no means universal, and
perhaps was even uncommon in the ninth century. The words
" Postea Eucharistia . . . quae per eodem (sic!) ministerium conse-
cratur" seem to mean that after the Mass, which followed the
actual Dedication, was finished, there was to be a deposition of the
Eucharist and relics, or of the Eucharist without relics, the deposition
in neither case being an integral part of the service.

Further, notwithstanding the general current in favour of the
cultus of the saints, there was a tendency in some parts of
the Church to observe the dangers connected with this veneration, ·
a danger apparently noticed by St. Athanasius, who records that
St. Antony would not allow his body to be kept, but desired that it
should be buried, and its place concealed (*vit. Anton.* 91), and who
himself bricked up relics given to him (Rufinus, *H. E.* ii. 28)[1].
The Emperors Gratian, Valentinian and Theodosius forbade the
trade in relics in A. D. 386 (*cod. Theod.* ix. 17, 7). In agreement
with this feeling of the greatest Egyptian theologian, the Coptic
Church has no ceremony of the burial of relics in its consecration
service, as I learn from Mr. G. Horner, who has kindly analyzed
the MS. recently given to me by the Coptic Patriarch[2]. The same
omission is observed in the old Irish form, described in a section
of the *Spotted Book* recently published by Mr. Olden. And,
according to Mr. E. S. Dewick[3], " in many English Pontificals there

[1] The motive is not quite clear. In the case of Athanasius it might partly be
to preserve the relics, in that of Antony we seem to discern something of the old
Egyptian desire to keep the body perfect. On Athanasius, again, and others
the polemic attacks of Julian might have some influence, and that a very proper
one. See S. Cyril *contra Jul.* vi. p. 204, ed. Span., and J., *Misopogon*, p. 361 B.

[2] This paper has been printed in the *Proc. Bibl. Arch. Soc.*, vol. xxi. pp. 86-107
(1899), and the MS. itself, I hope, will be printed by the *Henry Bradshaw Society*.

[3] See his paper *On a MS. Pontifical of a Bishop of Metz of the Fourteenth
Century* (reprinted from *Archæologia*, vol. liv. pp. 411-424), p. 6, note,
London, 1895. Mr. Dewick writes (30 Jan. 1899):—" I have looked at the
note in my paper on the Metz Pontifical, and I could wish that I had added
a few words. The statement should be :—' In many English Pontificals there
is no mention of the enclosing of the relics of saints in the sepulchre of the
altar, *as an essential part of the service*, and in one or two there is no mention
of relics at all.' In treating of English use there is no need to consider Leofric,
for the part referring to the dedication of a church is found in Leofric
A, which came from Lotharingia (see Warren's *Introduction*, p. xxvii). The

is no mention of the enclosing of the relics of saints in the sepulchre of the altar. When the enclosing of relics is noticed it is said to be done ' in the Roman manner' (*more Romano*), when no relics are enclosed the dedication is performed after the Anglican custom (*more Anglicano*)." Mr. Olden, commenting on the *Spotted Book*, suggests that the absence of the custom is due to the fact that the early British and Irish Churches only dedicated their churches to living saints. This is probably not so much the truth of the matter as that Celtic buildings were called after the Saint of the Monastery, living or dead, to which the land on which they stood belonged. The Roman idea was that a saint possessed the Church through being wholly or partly buried in it; the Celtic, if I rightly understand it, that it actually belonged to him or to his family or clan, i. e. his monks [1].

But over and above this distinction our forefathers, whether Celtic or Saxon or Norman, were intelligent enough to see the weak side of such a practice, and I should expect to find that the *mos Anglicanus* was one of the good customs which made the work of the Reformation easier in this country.

Certainly there is no mention of relics in the Pontifical office printed by Maskell, and ascribed by him to the Sarum Diocese, but

Pontificals of the tenth and eleventh centuries seem to regard the burial of relics as a separate service, and distinctly Roman. Thus Dunstan's Pontifical (from which Martene has taken his Ordo IV in *De Ant. Eccl. Rit.* ii. 257, Venetiis, 1783) has the relics in a separate section, ' Incipit ordo quomodo in sacra Romana ecclesia reliquiae condantur.' The expression *si sunt autem reliquiae* implies that they were not always used. Martene's Ordo III, which has also been printed by John Gage in *Archaeologia*, vol. xxv. p. 235, supplies similar evidence. The MS. in Cambridge University Library, Mm. iii. 21, used by Maskell in his *Monumenta Ritualia*, has no notice of the burial of relics in the portion printed by him. Lacy's Pontifical (ed. Barnes, p. 32) has a separate section on *Reconditio Reliquiarum*, but the words *Quando reliquie ponende sunt* seem to imply that it was not essential. But Brit. Mus. MS. Lansdowne 451 (a London Pontifical of the end of the fourteenth cent.) gives the clearest evidence, for it provides two alternative services, one, *mos Anglicanus* without relics, the other, *mos Romanus* with relics; and it is expressly added ' licet istis temporibus hoc raro fiat propter reliquiarum paucitatem et novorum sanctorum raram canonizationem.' "

[1] I think Mr. J. Willis Bund is probably right when he says:—" If a Church was called by the name of a saint it did not imply, as has been assumed, that the saint had founded it, or that it was dedicated to him by the founder. It merely implied that the church was built on land that had become by grant or otherwise the property of the monastery to which the saint belonged." *Celtic Church in Wales*, p. 322, 1897.

perhaps rather belonging to Lincoln: and in the xiii[th] century
Pontifical which belonged to Archbishop Bainbridge the only
reference is in a rubric which precedes a prayer in which the
name of the Saint of the Church is recited. The rubric runs as
follows: *Sequitur oratio dicenda sive reliquiae [fuerint] sive non* (ed.
Henderson for Surtees Soc., p. 74. Bainbridge's date is A.D.
1508–1514). This is important as showing that up to the eve of
the Reformation, the use of relics was optional, and perhaps more
often neglected than not.

The place in which relics were buried when they were used in
such a service, seems to have varied. It is sometimes described as
"in confessione," that is, strictly speaking, in the crypt or vault
under the altar (e. g. *Pont. of Egbert*, p. 46 and *Sacramentary of
Drogo of Metz*, ap. Duchesne, p. 467). Sometimes it is simply "in
ipso altario" (*Sacr. of Angoulême*, ib. 464). Sometimes relics, enclosed in a box, were inserted into holes cut in the surface of the slab
of the altar. There is a picture of this in B. M. Lansdowne 451. But
generally the idea was that the body of the martyr was "under the
altar," a thought brought into symbolic connexion with the passage
of the Apocalypse which speaks of souls in that position praying
for Christ's second coming to judgement (Apoc. vi. 9, cp. xvi. 7).
In connexion with this the Antiphon was generally sung: "Sub
altare Domini sedes accepistis: intercedite pro nobis apud quem
gloriari meruistis." This is found in the Egbert Pontifical (p. 46)
and in the ninth-century Sacramentary of Metz. No doubt to
popular devotion the body and the soul were both together in the
relic: and to visit a shrine and give a gift to it was actually to visit
the saint and present him with something valuable. Scholars may
remember the lines written by our countryman Ceolfrid when he
took the great Bible written in a Northumbrian monastery to the
shrine of St. Peter at Rome. He evidently felt that he was making
a gift to the prince of the Apostles himself. Indeed the false
position to which the Church of Rome has grown in Christendom
is to a considerable extent owing to its possessing the sepulchres,
and we may presume the bodies, of St. Peter and St. Paul. To
visit the "limina apostolorum" is a duty enjoined by oath on
Bishops of the Roman obedience to the present day, and "limen"
in this sense is a technical term, meaning the chapel in which a
martyr is buried; see Ducange, s. v.

Architects and antiquaries no doubt can supply instances of such relics or receptacles for relics still existing in England. Their comparative rarity is not due, I think, only to Reformation zeal, but to the fact that they were not so common here as elsewhere. I have learnt that at St. Phillack in Cornwall is a little recess grooved in the centre of the wall beneath the east window, which still contains a phial half-full of blood or some similar substance. At another Cornish Chapel (St. Clether or St. Cleer) there is a recess or ambry which appears to have held relics, under the stone altar belonging to a church older than the existing one which dates from the fifteenth century. At Madron Chapel near Penzance, there is a hole about four inches square in the centre of the altar slab. There are also recesses, presumably for relics, in the masonry on which the altar slab once rested in one of the Eastern Chapels of Castle Acre Priory in Norfolk[1]. These and similar instances are historically interesting. I trust, however, that nothing which I have said may tend in any measure or degree to a practical revival among us of the ceremonies of relic burial. They were at first introduced in parish churches, with not the best or most adequate motives, and the belief which they tend to encourage is often of a very material and, I may add, selfish kind. They are in no degree necessary to the full purpose of the consecration of a Church nor are they strictly English.

At the same time we have preserved the solemn naming of a church, and cannot be wrong in laying from time to time special stress both in prayer and sermon on the memory and good example which it brings home to us, and the fuller sense of the living reality of the communion of saints [2]. The Church of England does not call upon the saints and martyrs to pray for us individually, but it does not doubt that they join in our prayers for the whole Church. It does not ascribe a glory and a complete felicity to the martyrs for which it has no warrant in holy Scripture, but it calls upon the spirits and souls of the righteous to bless the Lord, with us, and to praise and magnify Him for ever.

---

[1] I owe the knowledge of these instances to the diligence of Professor Collins. There is a slab, not now, if ever, an altar, at Tarrant Rushton, Dorset, which has holes on its surface that have sometimes been supposed to have contained relics.

[2] See a good section on this subject in Hooker, *E. P.* v. 13.

Note on the Foundation-Sacrifice of Paganism.

On p. 20 I have written, " Relic burial may even have been in some degree a survival of the barbarous ' foundation-sacrifice' of paganism." What this was may be seen by reference to Jacob Grimm's *Teutonic Mythology*, E. T. by J. S. Stallybrass, vol. iii. 1141-4, vol. iv. 1646-7 (Lond. 1883 and 1888); Fr. Lenormant, *Les origines de l'histoire d'après la Bible*, i. chap. iv. *Le fratricide et la fondation de la première ville*, esp. pp. 143-8 (Paris, 1880) ; E. B. Tylor, *Primitive Culture*, i. pp. 104-8 (2d ed. Lond. 1873). The sacrifice consisted in burying alive a human victim, if possible innocent and most valuable (for which a lamb or horse was substituted in milder, and especially in Christian, ages), under any building which it was specially hoped might stand for a long period, or in smearing the foundation stones with its blood. The idea of this sacrifice seems to have been, as Mr. Tylor puts it (p. 106), "either to propitiate the earth-spirit with a victim, or to convert the soul of the victim himself into a protecting demon." The first idea seems the earlier. The second is a natural development of it, and is closely connected with the notions attaching to patron or tutelary saints. We may observe also the stress laid upon the bloody head dug up under the Capitol, and the bloody condition of the bodies of Gervasius and Protasius found by St. Ambrose, and other legends of blood exuding from relics. The Church did not of course mean to propitiate the earth-spirit by such burial, but it clung to the almost ineradicable superstition which connects the activity of the disembodied soul with the place of its burial, and it believed that the innocence or purity of the person buried lent a virtue and stability to the building.

The legend of the voluntary death and burial of St. Odran or Oran at Hy, in compliance with St. Columba's wish that his community might take root in the island, is closely connected with this superstition. See Reeves' *Adamnan*, note on iii. 6, p. 203 (Dublin, 1857).

List of Forms in use in the XVIIth Century.

1610. Bp. W. Barlow (Lincoln), Fulmire Church and Churchyard. Lamb. MS. 577, 185 and MS. 929, 83-4, and Stow ap. E. C. Harington, *On the Cons. of Churches*, Lond. 1848, 103.

1610-11. Bp. Barlow (Lincoln), Hatfield House Chapel[1]. Lambeth MS. 929, 86.

1615. Bp. King (London), Edmington. ⎫ Collier, *Ch. H.* bk. viii.
1616. Bp. Moreton (Chester), Clay Hall, ⎬ Harington, 116-8.
Barking. ⎭

1620. Bp. Andrewes (Winton), Jesus Chapel, Southampton. Harington, 145 ff.

1622. Bp. Monteigne (London), St. James', Duke's Place, Aldgate. Oughton, *Ordo Judiciorum*, ii. 265.

1622. Bp. Monteigne (London), Epping Chapel enlarged. Oughton, *O. J.*, ii. 282.

1624. Bp. Harsnett (Norwich), Churchyard of St. Margaret, King's Lynn. Norwich *Institution Book* xxi, Appendix.

1630. Bp. Laud (London), St. Katharine Creed (Rushworth, ii. 77). Harington, 109-110.

1631. Bp. Laud (London), Hammersmith. Oughton, *O. J.*, ii. 269.

1632. Bp. Laud (London), Stanmore Magna. Oughton, *O. J.*, ii. 249, Harington, 195-207.

1632. Bp. Laud (London), Private Chapel of Mr. Weston at Roehampton, by commission from Abp. Abbot. Abbot's *Register*, pt. 3, fol. 126 B.

1632. Bp. White (Ely), Peterhouse Chapel, Lambeth MS. 577, 193. Fuller Russell, p. 39 (see next entry).

1634. Bp. Theophilus Field (Hereford), Abbey Dore. Lambeth MS. 577, 113, and edited by Rev. John Fuller Russell, Lond. 1874.

1634. Abp. Neile (York), Leeds Chapel. Lambeth MS. 577, 149; Petition, *ib.* 26. Fuller Russell, l. c. p. 38.

1640? Dr. Cosin, *Corresp.*, ii. 81-83; Consecration of Churchyard.

1661. Form discussed in Convocation. Cardwell's *Synodalia*, ii.668,&c.

1665. Bp. Cosin (Durham), Auckland Castle Chapel. Lambeth MS. 929, 85.

[1] Another copy in Lambeth MS. 76, D. 6, at p. 363, with a note in Archbishop Laud's writing, 'Taken out of ye Register's Office and delivered unto me on Sunday, 12 Febr., 1637.'

1665. Bp. Cosin (Durham), Tynemouth. *Corresp.*, ii. 175-195.
NB. This is probably the form discussed in Convocation.

1666, &c. *Irish Form of Consecration of Churches.* Reprinted by
S.P.C.K., 1893.

1677. Bp. Gunning (Ely), Emmanuel College Chapel, Cambridge.
Lambeth MS. 639, 14.

1684. Bp. Compton (London), St. James' Chapel (Piccadilly). Lambeth MS. 74, H. 13, No. 7.

1685. Abp. Sancroft (Canterbury), Coleshill Plate. Lambeth MS. 577,
105. R. Tisdale, *The Form of Dedication or Consecration of
a Church or Chapel,* Lond. for John Hartley, 4to, 1703, cp.
James Owen, *History of the Consecration of Altars, Temples,
and Churches*, p. 86, Lond. 1706.

1697? Bp. Spratt (Rochester), Bromley College Chapel. Lambeth
MS. 929, 82.

THE FORM OF PRAYER

AND ORDER OF CEREMONIES USED AT

THE CONSECRATION OF CHURCHES, CHAPELS

AND BURIAL GROUNDS IN THE

DIOCESE OF SALISBURY.

Revised Edition with Music.

𝔅𝔶 𝔄𝔲𝔱𝔥𝔬𝔯𝔦𝔱𝔶.

[1898]

PREPARATIONS IN ORDER TO
THE CONSECRATION OF A CHURCH
[AND BURIAL GROUND].

¶ The Church is to be furnished with a Font of Stone and Cover, with a Vessel to bring water for Baptism, Pulpit, Stall or Stalls for the Clergy with Desks or Lecterns, Holy Table with Cushion or Desk for the Service Book, Hassocks or Kneeling Mats, suitable Seats both in the Nave and Chancel, Bier or Trestles with Pall, one or more Bells; the Ten Commandments, the ' Table of Kindred and Affinity, wherein whosoever are related are forbidden by Scripture and our Laws to marry together;' one large Bible, one Book of Common Prayer for the Minister's Desk, and another containing 'the Order of Holy Communion' for the Holy Table, a Book of Offices ; Register Books with Iron Chest for keeping the Registers; a Flagon, Chalice, Paten, and Alms-dish, a Covering for the Holy Table, Linen Cloth and Napkins for the same, and Surplices.

The Burial Ground is to be properly enclosed, fenced, and completed with Gates and Churchways.

¶ The Deed of Conveyance or Donation of the Ground, the Endowments and the Evidences thereof, the Nomination of the Minister, and such other Documents as shall in any case be requisite, are to be laid before the Bishop or his Chancellor some time before the day proposed for the Consecration of the Church, in order to the preparing of the Act or Sentence of the Consecration against that day.

¶ Notice of the Bishop's intention to consecrate the Church [and Burial Ground], with the day and hour appointed, is to be fixed on the Church door at least three days beforehand.

¶ If the Building is to be consecrated as a Chapel, in which some sacramental or religious Rites may not be solemnized, the same directions are to be observed, except with regard to a Font, Bier, Register Books, and other articles not required for the service in the Chapel.

¶ Chairs are to be set on the north side of the Holy Table for the Bishop, on the south side for the Chaplains, and one conveniently near the Bishop's chair, but without the Sanctuary, for the Chancellor.

Thanks are due for the Music to Rev. H. W. Carpenter, M.A., Precentor of Salisbury Cathedral, and to Mr. W. S. Bambridge, Mus. Bac. Oxon., Organist of Marlborough College, Wilts.

THE FORM AND ORDER OF CONSECRATION.

—++—

¶ The Bishop, attended by his Chaplains, shall be received at the entrance of the Churchyard, or at the West Door, or some other principal entrance of the Church, by the Minister and Clergy in their Surplices, the Churchwardens and some of the principal Inhabitants, including, if possible, the Patron or Patrons of the Church. Here a Petition, signed by the Incumbent and Church-wardens, Patron, Trustees, or others, as the case may require, shall be delivered to the Bishop by some fit person in the name of those present, praying that he will consecrate the Church [and the Burial Ground thereto belonging], to which he will make a suitable reply.

¶ A procession will then be formed, and, when it is possible, will make a complete circuit of the Church, saying or singing one or more of the following Psalms: lxviii. *Exurgat Deus*, lxxxiv. *Quam dilecta!*, cxxi. *Levavi oculos*, cxxii. *Laetatus sum*, cxxvii. *Nisi Dominus*, cxxxii. *Memento Domine*. Appropriate Hymns may be added with the approval of the Bishop. [Where a Burial Ground is to be Consecrated, the Procession may begin by making a circuit of the ground, singing first one or more of the above-named Psalms and then one or more of the following: xvi. *Conserva me, Domine*, xxiii. *Dominus regit me*, xlix. *Audite haec, omnes*, cxv. *Non nobis, Domine*, cxxxix. *Domine, probasti*, and then will follow the circuit of the Church.]

————————

¶ *After making a circuit of the Church the Procession shall halt at the West Door, or other principal Entrance, and shall stand apart, forming into two lines so as to allow the Bishop with his Chaplains to reach the Door.*

Then shall the Bishop say :

Let us pray.   Lord have mercy upon us.

Answer.

Christ have mercy upon us.   Lord have mercy up-on   us.

Our Father, which art in heaven, Hallowed be ·
Thy Name, Thy kingdom come, Thy will be
done, in earth as it is in heaven.   Give us this
day our daily bread, And forgive us our trespasses, As we forgive them that trespass against
us ; And lead us not into temptation, But deliver us from evil.   For Thine is the kingdom,
The power, and the glory, For ever and ever.   A - men.

O LORD, our King and God, who hast ordered and constituted the hosts of Angels and Archangels in Heaven to
minister to Thy glory, grant that, as we enter this House, Thy
holy Angels may enter with us as fellow-servants in our worship,
and may join with us in glorifying Thy goodness; for Thine is all
glory, honour and worship, O Father, Son and Holy Ghost, now
and for ever.   *Amen.*

*The Bishop will then take his Pastoral Staff in his right hand,
and knock three times upon the closed door, saying :*

Lift up your heads, O ye gates,} doors: {and the King} come in.
and be ye lift up, ye everlasting} {of glory shall }

Answer shall be made from within by the people:

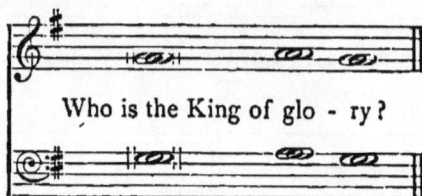

Who is the King of glo - ry?

The Bishop shall answer:

It is the Lord strong and mighty; it is the Lord mighty ⎫
in battle; even the Lord of hosts, He is the King of ⎭ glo - ry.

*Then shall the doors be opened wide and the keys be delivered
to the Bishop, who shall enter, followed by the Procession.*

Then the Bishop, standing near the west end of the Church, shall say:

Peace be to this House from God our heavenly Father.
Peace be to this House from His Son who is our Peace.
Peace be to this House from the Holy Ghost the Comforter.

Then the Bishop shall say this Antiphon:

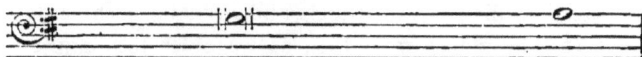

The Organ will give G.

Lift up your heads, O ye gates, and be ye ⎫
lift up, ye everlasting   ⎭ doors :

Answer.

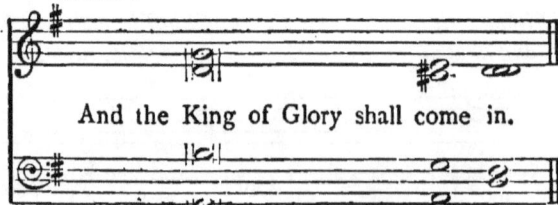

And the King of Glory shall come in.

c

Then shall the procession walk through the Church from West to East, singing PSALM xxiv., Domini est terra :

THE earth is the Lord's and all that therein is : the compass of the world, and they that dwell therein.

2. For he hath founded it upon the seas : and prepared it upon the floods.

3. Who shall ascend into the hill of the Lord : or who shall rise up in his holy place?

4. Even he that hath clean hands and a pure heart : and that ·hath not lift up his mind unto vanity, nor sworn to deceive his neighbour.

5. He shall receive the blessing from the Lord : and righteousness from the God of his salvation.

6. This is the generation of them that seek him : even of them that seek thy face, O Jacob.

7. Lift up your heads, O ye gates, and be ye lift up, ye everlasting doors : and the King of Glory shall come in.

8. Who is the King of Glory : it is the Lord, strong and mighty, even the Lord mighty in battle.

9. Lift up your heads, O ye gates, and be ye lift up, ye everlasting doors : and the King of Glory shall come in.

10. Who is the King of Glory : even the Lord of hosts, he is the King of Glory.

Glory be to the Father, and to the Son : and to the Holy Ghost.

As it was in the beginning, is now, and ever shall be : world without end. Amen.

Then the Bishop, Clergy and Choir shall sing all together:

Lift up your heads, O ye gates, and be ye lift up, ye everlasting} doors : {and the King of Glory shall} come in.

¶ *The Bishop shall then lay the keys upon the Table which is to be hallowed, and, standing before it, shall say:*

O Lord Jesu Christ, who art the beginning and the ending of all things, the first and the last, who hast the key of the house of David, who openest and no man shutteth, who shuttest and no man openeth, give Thy power, we pray Thee, to us Thy servants, and grant that this house, now opened for Thy service, may alway be filled with Thy presence, and may ever remain a refuge for Thy faithful people, who with the Father and the Holy Ghost livest and reignest one God for ever and ever.　　A - men.

Then shall the Bishop kneel down, with his Chaplains behind him on either hand in front of the Table, and the Congregation shall be desired to keep silence for a space, for prayer on behalf of the Church to be hallowed, after which the hymn, Veni Creator Spiritus, *shall be sung.*

To be sung in Unison. No 157, Hymns A. and M.

1 Come, Holy Ghost, our souls inspire,
And lighten with celestial fire;
Thou the anointing Spirit art,
Who dost Thy sevenfold gifts impart.

2 Thy blessèd unction from above
Is comfort, life, and fire of love;
Enable with perpetual light
The dulness of our blinded sight.

3 Anoint and cheer our soilèd face
With the abundance of Thy grace;
Keep far our foes, give peace at home:
Where Thou art Guide no ill can come.

4 Teach us to know the Father, Son,
And Thee, of Both, to be but One:
That through the ages all along
This may be our endless song:

Praise . . . to Thy e - ter - nal me - rit,

Fa - ther, Son, and Ho - ly Spi - rit.

A . - men.

The Bishop's Chaplains will then say this Litany:

*[The Chaplains' part may be in monotone or with the
following ending throughout.]*

Stretch out Thine hand upon us, O Lord, }
and save us, pity us, raise us up } and de-fend us.

Answer.

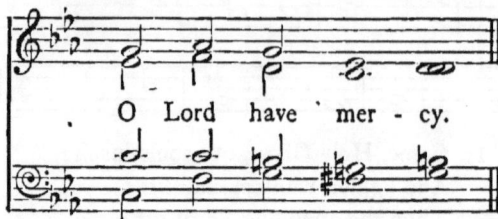

O Lord have mer - cy.

Let us pray in the peace of God.

Answer. O Lord have mercy.

Let us pray for the peace that cometh from above, and for the salvation of our souls.

Answer. O Lord have mercy.

Let us pray for the peace of the whole world, for the welfare of the Churches of God, and for the union of them all.

Answer. O Lord have mercy.

Let us pray for the conversion of those in unbelief and error, and especially for the ancient people of God.

Answer. O Lord have mercy.

Let us pray for our Country, our City and Diocese, and for all the churches of Christ within it.

Answer. O Lord have mercy.

Let us pray for all Christian people throughout the world.

Answer. O Lord have mercy.

Let us pray for the Bishops and Clergy of Christ's Church, especially for ———— Archbishop of Canterbury and for ———— Bishop of this Diocese.

Answer. O Lord have mercy.

Let us pray for all Christian princes and governors, especially our Sovereign Lady Queen Victoria.

Answer. O Lord have mercy.

Let us pray for the Rulers of this land, especially for those who bear office in this City [County].

Answer. O Lord have mercy.

Let us pray for the work of our hands and for all our brethren who are present with us.

Answer. O Lord have mercy.

Let us pray that this House and Sanctuary of ———— may be hallowed by the presence and power of the Holy Spirit.

Answer. O Lord have mercy.

Let us pray for all who travel by land or by water, especially for all in our colonies and in heathen lands, that their faith may increase and their good example strengthen the Church in the countries where they may sojourn.

Answer. O Lord have mercy.

Let us pray for all who are sick or suffering in mind, body or estate.

Answer. O Lord have mercy.

Let us pray for a holy and a happy death, for rest in paradise, and for the perfect vision of Thy glory.

Answer. O Lord have mercy.

Let us pray that we might follow Thy blessed saints and martyrs in bearing our cross before the world, and in advancing the honour of Thy kingdom.

Answer. O Lord have mercy.

Then shall the Bishop rise and say this prayer, the rest still kneeling:

Let us pray.

O GOD, who art from eternity to eternity, who hast made all things of nothing, who dwellest in light unapproachable and hast heaven for Thy throne and earth for Thy footstool; who gavest to Moses an ordinance and pattern, and didst fill Bezaleel with the spirit of wisdom, and didst endue them with power to prepare the Tabernacle of witness, wherein were ordinances of worship, the figures and symbols of the truth; who gavest to Solomon wisdom and largeness of heart and by his hand didst set up Thine ancient Temple; who didst teach Thy holy and glorious Apostles the service which is in the Spirit and the consecration of the true Tabernacle, and by their hand didst plant Churches and Sanctuaries in all the earth; who also hast permitted this House to be built under the name of _____, to Thy glory and that of Thy Son and Holy Spirit: Remember Thine eternal mercies, O immortal and gracious King, and abhor not us who are defiled with many sins, and break not Thy covenant by reason of our uncleanness, but forgive our trespasses, and strengthen us, by Thy grace and the presence of Thy Holy Spirit, rightly to perform the dedication of this House, and the consecration of this its Sanctuary. Yea, O Lord, our God and Saviour, hearken to us sinners and send down Thine All-holy Spirit, and sanctify this House for common prayer and praise, for the reading of holy Scriptures, for the ministry of Thy Word and Sacraments, for offering to Thy glorious Majesty the spiritual sacrifices of Thy Church, for blessing the people in Thy Name and for the performance of all holy ordinances. Fill it with everlasting light: choose it for Thy dwelling-place: make it an habitation of Thy glory: adorn it with Thy divine and supernatural gifts: make it a haven for the tempest-tossed, a place of healing for sufferers, a refuge for the sick, a defence against evil spirits. Let Thine eyes be open upon it day and night, and Thine ears be attentive to the prayer of those who enter it with fear and reverence to call upon Thy Name; and mercifully grant whatsoever they shall ask in faith. Let this House stand firm as long as time shall last; and make its Sanctuary a shrine of Thine indwelling Glory, so that the mystical sacrifices of Thy faithful people here offered unto Thee may be joined to the service and worship of Heaven, and be instruments of the grace of Thine overshadowing Presence, not through the ministry of our unworthy hands, but through Thine unspeakable Goodness.

Then shall be sung by the Bishop, Clergy, and Choir:

For Thou, Lord, art holy, and dwellest in the ho - ly,

Thou lovest them that love Thee, and suffer as witnesses } for Thee:

To Thee we offer up our praises and thanks - giv - ings,

Father, Son, and Ho - ly Ghost,

For ever and for ev - er. A - - men.

¶ *After this the Bishop with his Staff-bearer and Chaplains and the Minister of the Church shall proceed solemnly to the Font and to the other appointed places, at which they shall say the following prayers. The sentences of holy Scripture before each prayer shall be sung by the Choir and People.*

At the Font. TITUS iii. 5–7.

Not by works of righteousness which we have done, but according to His mercy He saved us, by the washing of regeneration and renewing of the Holy Ghost, which He shed on us abundantly - - - - - -

through Je - sus Christ our Sa - - viour;

that being justified by His Grace, we should be made
heirs according - - - - - - - -

to the hope of e - ter - nal life.

REGARD, O Lord, the supplications of this Thy congregation; and bless this Font, which we now hallow for Thy service, that it may be a laver of the new birth for all who shall be baptized herein; and grant that they, being washed and sanctified with the Holy Ghost, may die to sin and rise with Christ unto righteousness, and ever remain in the number of Thy faithful and elect children; through the same Jesus Christ our Lord. *Amen.*

At the Chancel Steps. 2 COR. i. 21, 22.

Now He that stablisheth us with you in Christ and hath
anointed us in God; Who hath also sealed us, and
given the - - - - - - - - - -

earn - est of the Spi - rit in our hearts.

GRANT, O Lord, that all who in this place shall renew the promises and vows of their Baptism, may be confirmed and strengthened with power from on high, and, receiving the sevenfold gift of the Holy Ghost, may continue Thine for ever, and daily increase in Thy Holy Spirit more and more, until they come to Thy everlasting kingdom, through Jesus Christ our Lord. *Amen.*

GEN. ii. 18.

The Lord God said, It is not good that the man should be alone; I will make - - - - - - - - -

him an help meet for him.

GRANT, O Lord, that they who shall be joined together in this place in the holy estate of Matrimony, may faithfully perform and keep the vow and covenant betwixt them made, and remain in perfect love and peace together unto their lives' end. *Amen.*

At the Lectern. 2 TIM. iii. 16, 17.

All Scripture is given by inspiration of God, and is profitable for doctrine, for reproof, for correction, for instruction in righteousness : that the man of God may be perfect, -

thorough-ly fur-nish'd un - to all good works.

GRANT, O Lord, that all who in this place shall read the Scriptures, which Thou hast given us, may be filled with the faith of Thy Gospel and with thankfulness to Thee, who dost reveal Thyself to men by the Word of Life, and may so read that all shall understand; and grant that all who hear may receive that Word into honest and good hearts, and may bring forth fruit with patience, through Jesus Christ our Lord. *Amen.*

At the Pulpit. 2 TIM. iv. 2, 5.

Preach the word; be instant in season, out of season, reprove, rebuke, exhort, with all - - - - - -

long suf - fer - ing and doc - trine.

Watch thou in all things; endure afflictions; do the work of an evangelist; - - - - - - - - -

make full proof of thy min - is - try.

GRANT, O Lord, that all who in this place shall preach Thy Word may be so filled with Thy Holy Spirit, that their wisdom and fervent zeal may turn back the hearts of sinners and establish the faith of all Thy children, through Jesus Christ our Lord. *Amen.*

At the Stalls of the Clergy. I PET. iv. 10.

As every man hath received the gift, even so minister the same one to another, as good stewards - - - -

of the ma - ni - fold grace of God.

GRANT, O Lord, that all who in this place shall minister to Thee may ever be mindful of the dignity of the office to which they are called, and that their prayers and praises may lead Thy people to the throne of grace, and be joined to the perpetual intercession of our great High Priest and Advocate with Thee, through the same Jesus Christ our Lord. *Amen.*

At the Choir Seats. I COR. xiv. 15, and PS. xcii. 1.

I will sing with the spirit and I will sing with the under-standing also. It is a good thing to give thanks unto the Lord and to - - - - - - - - -

sing prais - es un - to Thy

Name, O Thou most High - est.

G RANT, O Lord, that all who in this place shall sing to Thee may be filled with reverence, humility, and joy, and may draw the hearts of all who worship with them to long for the fruition of Thine unknown and eternal glories, through Jesus Christ our Lord. *Amen.*

At the Sanctuary steps. I COR. x. 16.

The cup of blessing which we bless is it not

the Com - mu - nion of the Blood of Christ?

The bread which we break - - is it not

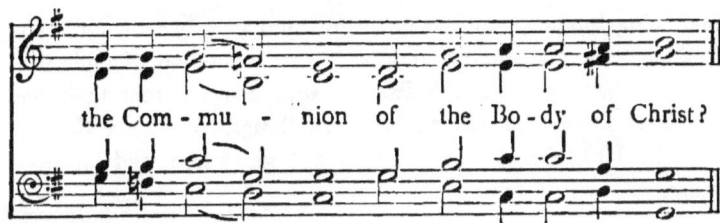

the Com - mu - nion of the Bo - dy of Christ?

Before the Lord's Table.

ALMIGHTY GOD, our heavenly Father, Who hast given Thy Son our Saviour Jesus Christ not only to die for us but also to be our spiritual food and sustenance in the Holy Sacrament of His Body and Blood, bless, we pray Thee, and hallow this Table as Thine own, for the purposes of that heavenly mystery; and grant that the memorial of His death may here be made with reverence and godly fear, and the sacrifice of praise and thanksgiving be offered with holiness and joy, to the honour of Thy glorious Name, the benefit of Thy whole Church, and the comfort of souls that shall live by feeding upon Him, through the same Jesus Christ our Lord, to whom with Thee and the Holy Ghost be all honour and glory world without end. *Amen.*

¶ *The Ornaments, holy Vessels, and fair linen Cloths shall then be presented to the Bishop by the Minister of the Church, to be placed over or upon the holy Table, the Bishop saying as he receives them:*

Be ye clean ye that bear the vessels of the Lord.

Answer. I will wash my hands in innocency, O Lord, and so will I go to Thine altar.

Then the Bishop shall say the following prayers:

O LORD, we beseech Thee of Thy merciful goodness to accept these offerings that we make, not of our own but of Thine, for all things come of Thee, and of Thine own do we give Thee: and grant that these vessels, which neither art nor costliness can make meet for the service of Thy holy mysteries, may ever be hallowed by Thy blessing, through Jesus Christ our Lord. *Amen.*

GRANT, O Lord, that they who shall receive in this place the blessed Sacrament of the Body and Blood of Christ, may come to that holy mystery, with faith, charity, and true repentance;

and being fulfilled with Thy grace and heavenly benediction, may,
to their great and endless comfort, obtain remission of their sins,
and all other benefits of His Passion, who died and rose again and
ascended for us that He might fill all things, to whom with Thee
and the Holy Ghost be all honour and glory now and for evermore. *Amen.*

¶ *Then he shall turn to the people, and the Clergy, Choir, and People
shall sing with him:*

Christ hath reconciled us unto God in one body by the Cross,

hav - ing slain the en - mi - ty there - by.

Sure - ly the Lord is in this place.

This is none other than } this is the gate of Heaven.
the House of God and

Then the Bishop shall say the following prayers:

GRANT, O Lord, that those Thy servants who shall come into this Thy holy Temple, may remember that they are themselves Temples of the Holy Ghost, eschewing all things contrary to their profession, and following all such things as are agreeable to the same. *Amen.*

GRANT that all wandering thoughts, all carnal and worldly imaginations, may be far from them; and all godly and spiritual meditations may come in their place, and may daily be renewed and grow in them. *Amen.*

GRANT, when they pray, that their prayers may ascend up into Thy presence, as the incense; and the lifting up of their hands be as the daily sacrifice. Purify their hearts, sanctify their spirits, and fulfil all their minds, that what they faithfully ask they may effectually obtain, and ever give thanks unto Thee. *Amen.*

GRANT, when they offer, that their Alms of Christian love, and their Oblations for the service of Thy Sanctuary, may come up as a memorial before Thee; and they may feel and know that with such sacrifices Thou art well pleased. *Amen.*

GRANT that this whole place which is here dedicated to Thee by our office and ministry may also be hallowed by the sanctifying power of Thy Holy Spirit and so for ever continue through Thy mercy, O blessed Lord God, who dost live and govern all things world without end. *Amen.*

NOW unto the King eternal, immortal, invisible, the only wise God, the Father, the Son, and the Holy Ghost, be honour, and glory, for ever and ever. *Amen.*

Then shall be said or sung by the Bishop, Clergy, Choir and People:

Behold a ladder set up on the earth, and the top of it } reach-ed to Heaven;

and behold the Angels of } and de-scend-ing on it.
God ascending }

Sure - ly · the Lord is in this place.

· This is none other than } this is the gate of Heaven.
the House of God and }

[¶ *Where a Burial Ground is to be consecrated the Bishop with his Chaplains shall then proceed outside the Church, preceded by the Churchwardens and followed by the Clergy and Choir, and shall stand in the centre of the ground or in some other convenient place. The Clergy and Choir shall arrange themselves half on one side and the other half on the other side of him. Then the Bishop taking his Pastoral Staff in his left hand shall say:*

Yea, though I walk through the valley of the } e - vil.
shadow of Death, I will fear no }

Answer.

For thou art with me; thy rod and thy staff com - fort me.

D

Bishop.

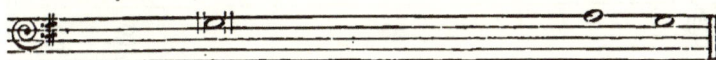

For why? thou shalt not leave my soul in hell, }
neither shalt thou suffer thy holy one to see cor- } rup - tion.

Answer.

But they that run after another god shall have great trou - ble.

Bishop.

But as for me, I will behold thy presence in right - eous - ness.

Answer.

And when I awake up after thy likeness I shall }
be satisfied - - - - - - - } with it.

Bishop.

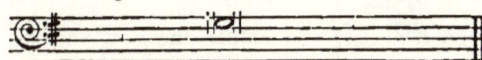

The Lord be with you.

Answer.

pp. slowly. And with thy Spir - it.

Let us pray.

Our Father, which art in heaven, Hallowed be
Thy Name, Thy kingdom come, Thy will be
done, in earth as it is in heaven. Give us this
day our daily bread, And forgive us our trespasses, As we forgive them that trespass
against us; And lead us not into temptation,
But deliver us from evil.   A - men.

Then shall he say this Collect:

O. LORD Jesu Christ, Who art the resurrection and the life,
Who by Thy death hast overcome death, and by Thy
rising again hast opened to us the gate of everlasting life, Who
shall send Thine angels and gather Thine elect from all the ends
of the earth: We humbly beseech Thee for all those whose bodies
shall here be committed to the ground, that they may rest in the hope
of resurrection to eternal life through Thee, O blessed Lord God,
Who shalt change their vile bodies, that they may be like unto Thy
glorious body, according to the mighty working whereby Thou art
able to bring all things into subjection to Thyself; Who livest and
reignest with the Father and the holy Spirit, one God world without
end. *Amen.*

¶ *Then shall he bless the ground:*

THE blessing of God Almighty, the Father, the Son, and the
Holy Ghost, be ever upon this place, and sanctify and
keep it holy, that it may be a fit resting place for the bodies of His
saints, until the day of the Lord Jesus, when He shall come to
judge the quick and the dead, and the world by fire. *Amen.*

¶ *After this the procession shall return into the Church, and the
Bishop shall return to the Sanctuary.*]

¶ *Then shall the Bishop seat himself in his Chair, and order the
sentence of Consecration to be read by the Chancellor or his deputy,
the people standing. Which done the Bishop shall sign the sentence
and declare the Church to be consecrated and order the document to*

be enrolled and preserved in the muniments of the Registry of the Diocese.

¶ *An Anthem or Hymn shall here be sung, during which those who do not desire to remain for Holy Communion are requested quietly to leave the Church.*

¶ *Then shall follow the Office for the Holy Communion.*

The Collects.

O MOST glorious Lord God, we acknowledge that we are not worthy to offer unto Thee anything belonging to us; yet we beseech Thee, of Thy great goodness, graciously to accept the dedication of this place to Thy service, and to prosper this our undertaking; Receive the prayers and intercessions of us, and all others Thy servants, who, either now, or hereafter, entering into this House, shall call upon Thee; and give both them and us grace to prepare our hearts to serve Thee with reverence and Godly fear. Fill us with an awful apprehension of Thy Divine Majesty, and a deep sense of our own unworthiness; that so approaching Thy sanctuary with lowliness and devotion, and coming before Thee with clean thoughts and pure hearts, with bodies undefiled and minds sanctified, we may always perform a service acceptable to Thee, through Jesus Christ our Lord. *Amen.*

B LESSED be Thy Name, O Lord, that it hath pleased Thee to put into the hearts of Thy *servants* . . . . to erect this House to Thy honour and worship. Bless, O Lord, them, their families, and substance, and accept the works of their hand: remember them concerning this; wipe not out this kindness that they have shewed for the House of their God, and the offices thereof; and grant that all who shall enjoy the benefit of this pious work, may show forth their thankfulness by making a right use of it, to the glory of Thy blessed Name, through Jesus Christ our Lord. *Amen.*

O EVERLASTING God, Who hast ordained and constituted the services of Angels and men in a wonderful order; Mercifully grant, that as Thy holy Angels alway do Thee service in heaven, so, by Thy appointment, they may succour and defend us on earth; through Jesus Christ our Lord. *Amen.*

Then shall follow the Collect for the Day and the Collect for the Festival connected with the name of the Church.

The Epistle. 1 St. Peter ii. 1—10.

WHEREFORE laying aside all malice, and all guile and hypocrisies, and envies, and all evil speakings, as newborn babes, desire the sincere milk of the word, that ye may grow thereby: if so be ye have tasted that the Lord is gracious. To whom coming, as unto a living stone, disallowed indeed of men, but chosen of God, and precious, ye also, as lively stones, are built up a spiritual house, an holy priesthood, to offer up spiritual sacrifices, acceptable to God by Jesus Christ. Wherefore also it is contained in the scripture, Behold, I lay in Sion a chief corner stone, elect, precious: and he that believeth on him shall not be confounded. Unto you therefore which believe he is precious: but unto them which be disobedient, the stone which the builders disallowed, the same is made the head of the corner, and a stone of stumbling, and a rock of offence, even to them which stumble at the word, being disobedient: whereunto also they were appointed. But ye are a chosen generation, a royal priesthood, an holy nation, a peculiar people; that ye should show forth the praises of him who hath called you out of darkness into his marvellous light: which in time past were not a people, but are now the people of God: which had not obtained mercy, but now have obtained mercy.

Or this. Rev. xxi. 1—14.

I SAW a new heaven and a new earth: for the first heaven and the first earth were passed away; and there was no more sea. And I John saw the holy city, new Jerusalem, coming down from God out of heaven, prepared as a bride adorned for her husband. And I heard a great voice out of heaven saying, Behold, the tabernacle of God is with men, and he will dwell with them, and they shall be his people, and God himself shall be with them, and be their God. And God shall wipe away all tears from their eyes; and there shall be no more death, neither sorrow, nor crying, neither shall there be any more pain: for the former things have passed away. And he that sat upon the throne said, Behold, I make all things new. And he said unto me, Write; for these words are true and faithful. And he said unto me, It is done. I am Alpha and Omega, the beginning and the end. I will give unto him that is athirst of the fountain of the water of life freely. He that overcometh shall inherit all things; and I will be his God, and he shall be my son. But the fearful, and unbelieving, and the abominable, and murderers, and whoremongers, and sorcerers, and idolaters, and all liars, shall have their part in the lake which burneth with fire and brimstone : which is the second death. And there came unto me one of the seven angels which had the seven vials full of the seven last plagues, and talked with me, saying, Come hither, I will shew thee the bride, the Lamb's wife. And he carried me away in the spirit to a great and high mountain, and shewed me that great city, the holy Jerusalem, descending out of heaven from God, having the glory of God : and her light was like unto a stone most precious, even like a jasper stone, clear as crystal; and had a wall great and high, and had twelve gates, and at the gates twelve angels, and names written thereon which are the names of the twelve tribes of the children of Israel : on the east three gates; on the north three gates; on the south three gates; and on the west three gates. And the wall of the city had twelve foundations, and in them the names of the twelve apostles of the Lamb.

The Gospel. St. MATTHEW xxi. 12—16.

JESUS went into the temple of God, and cast out all them that sold and bought in the temple, and overthrew the tables of the moneychangers, and the seats of them that sold doves, and said unto them, It is written, My house shall be called the house of prayer; but ye have made it a den of thieves. And the blind and the lame came to him in the temple; and he healed them. And when the chief priests and scribes saw the wonderful things that he did, and the children crying in the temple, and saying, Hosanna to the Son of David ; they were sore displeased, and said unto him, Hearest thou what these say ? And Jesus saith unto them, Yea ; have ye never read, Out of the mouth of babes and sucklings thou hast perfected praise ?

Or this. St. JOHN ii. 13—22.

THE Jews' passover was at hand, and Jesus went up to Jeru- salem, and found in the temple those that sold oxen and sheep and doves, and the changers of money sitting : and when he had made a scourge of small cords, he drove them all out of the temple, and the sheep, and the oxen ; and poured out the changers' money, and overthrew the tables ; and said unto them that sold doves, Take these things hence ; make not my Father's house an house of merchandise. And his disciples remembered that it was written, The zeal of thine house hath eaten me up. Then answered the Jews and said unto him, What sign shewest thou unto us, seeing that thou doest these things? Jesus answered and said unto them, Destroy this temple and in three days I will raise it up. Then said the Jews, Forty and six years was this temple in building, and wilt thou rear it up in three days? But he spake of the temple of his body. When therefore he was risen from the dead, his disciples remembered that he had said this unto them ; and they believed the scripture, and the word which Jesus had said.

¶ *After the* Gloria in Excelsis *the Bishop shall add :*

O ETERNAL Lord God, who holdest all souls in life, we beseech Thee to shed forth upon Thy whole Church in Paradise and on earth the bright beams of Thy light and heavenly comfort; and grant that we, following the good examples of those who have served Thee here and are at rest, may with them at length enter into Thine unending joy, through Jesus Christ our Lord. *Amen.*

THE BLESSING.

Collects which may be used on certain days.

St. Patrick, Apostle of Ireland (17 *March*, 465 ?).

O GOD who didst teach Thy servant PATRICK to love the land of his captivity and willingly to spend and be spent that he might bring its people unto Thee : grant that in all our troubles we may hear Thy voice, and gladly learn what Thou wouldest have us to do, through Jesus Christ our Lord. *Amen.*

St. George (23 *April*, 303).

O LORD God of hosts, who didst give grace to Thy servant GEORGE to lay aside the fear of man and to confess Thee even unto death, grant that we, and all our countrymen who bear office in the world, may think lightly of earthly place and honour, and seek rather to please the Captain of our salvation, who hath chosen us to be His soldiers, to whom with Thee and the Holy Ghost be thanks and praise from all the armies of Thy Saints now and for evermore. *Amen.*

St. Aldhelm, first Bishop of Sherborne (25 *May*, 709).

O GOD who hast made man's lips to praise Thee, and givest skill to his hands, we thank Thee for Thy servant ALDHELM, whom Thou didst instruct to be a teacher of Thy people in this Diocese; and we pray Thee to continue a full supply of faithful and learned men for Thy service in every age, through Jesus Christ our Lord. *Amen.*

St. Augustine, first Archbishop of Canterbury (26 *May*, 605).

O LORD, who hast taught us in Thy holy word that Kings shall be the nursing fathers of Thy Church and their Queens her nursing mothers, we thank Thee for the preaching of Thy servant AUGUSTINE, by whose zeal and devotion the Kingdom of England received the Gospel, whereby we have been brought out of darkness and error to the clear light and true knowledge of Thee and of Thy Son: to whom with Thee and the Holy Ghost be all glory, praise and thanksgiving now and for ever. *Amen.*

St. Boniface (5 *June*, 755).

O LORD Jesu Christ, who callest to Thee whom Thou willest and sendest them whither Thou dost choose, we thank Thee for calling Thy servant BONIFACE from our own West-Saxon land, and for sending him to be the Apostle of Germany and to die for the faith in Frisia: and we humbly pray Thee to raise up among us faithful men in this our day to go forth to destroy the strong-holds of idolatry and to build up Thy Church in heathen lands: . who livest and reignest with the Father and the Holy Spirit one God world without end. *Amen.*

St. Alban, first Martyr in Britain (17 *June*, 303).

O MERCIFUL Saviour, who dost teach us that those who receive Thy ministers have the blessing of receiving Thee, we thank Thee for the example of Thy martyr St. ALBAN, to whom Thou didst thus reveal Thyself in days of persecution; and we pray Thee that Thy clergy and people may ever be ready to bear witness together unto death: who with the Father and the Holy Spirit art one God for evermore. *Amen.*

. *St. Mary Magdalen* (22 *July*).

M ERCIFUL Father, give us grace, that we never presume to sin through the example of any creature, but if it shall chance us at any time to offend Thy divine majesty, that then we may truly repent, and lament the same, after the example of MARY MAGDALENE, and by lively faith obtain remission of all our sins: through the only merits of Thy Son our Saviour Christ. *Amen.*

The Transfiguration of our Lord (6 August).

O GOD, who didst call the Saints of the old Covenant to bear witness to THY SON'S TRANSFIGURATION, and by a voice from the cloud of light didst bid us hearken unto Him : grant that, as we have found Him in deed the only perfect Teacher of the Truth, so we may one day behold Him face to face in glory : who liveth and reigneth, with Thee and the Holy Ghost, one God, world without end. *Amen.*

St. Cyprian, Bishop of Carthage (14 or 26 September, 258).

O GOD, who didst give grace to Thy Bishop CYPRIAN to consecrate all his powers to the service of Thy Church in Africa, and to build and guard it in troublous times: grant to all those who bear rule in Thy house to think ever of its glory, its purity, and its beauty, and to welcome death with thanksgiving whensoever Thou shalt send it ; through Jesus Christ our Lord. *Amen.*

St. Martin, Bishop of Tours in France (11 November, 397).

O LORD, who didst teach Thy servant St. MARTIN to follow Thee as a boy, and to serve Thee unweariedly through length of days : Grant to Thy Pastors to be like him in discerning the tokens of Thy presence, in showing zeal for Thy glory and gentleness towards those who have gone astray, that they may draw the nations closer to Thyself; who with the Father and the Holy Ghost livest and reignest one God world without end. *Amen.*

St. Hugh, Bishop of Lincoln (17 November, 1200).

O MERCIFUL Father, who didst endow Thy servant HUGH of Lincoln with a wise and cheerful boldness and didst teach him how to commend the discipline of holy life to Kings and Princes : Give us grace not only to be bold, but to have just cause for boldness, even the fear and love of Thyself alone. Grant this, O Father, for the sake of Thy dear Son, our Lord and Saviour Jesus Christ. *Amen.*

St. Clement, Bishop of Rome (23 November, 100).

O LORD, who in every age dost write names in Thy book of life, and dost lead the meek of the earth to be followers of the Lamb of God : Raise up to us teachers, like Thy servant CLEMENT, the disciple of Thy first Apostles, who by their writings may instruct the Church without thought of self, and open to us healing fountains of repentance, peace and love : through the same Jesus Christ our Lord. *Amen.*

OXFORD: HORACE HART
PRINTER TO THE UNIVERSITY

PUBLICATIONS

OF THE

Society for Promoting Christian Knowledge.

———◦+◦———

	s.	d.

Alone with God; or, Helps to Thought and Prayer.
For the Use of the Sick; based on short passages of
Scripture. By the Rev. F. BOURDILLON, M.A., Author
of "Lesser Lights." 12mo. ....*Cloth boards* 1 0

Being of God, Six Addresses on the.
By C. J. ELLICOTT, D.D., Bishop of Gloucester and Bristol.
Small post 8vo.................................*Cloth boards* 1 6

**Bible Places; or, The Topography of the Holy
Land.**
By the Rev. Canon TRISTRAM. New Edition, brought
up to date. With Map and numerous Woodcuts.
Crown 8vo.................................*Half bound* 5 0

Called to be Saints.
The Minor Festivals Devotionally Studied. By the late
CHRISTINA G. ROSSETTI. Printed on hand-made paper.
Top edge gilt. Crown 8vo. ....*Buckram boards* 5 0

Christians under the Crescent in Asia.
By the Rev. E. L. CUTTS, B.A., Author of "Turning-
Points of Church History," &c. With numerous Illus-
trations. Crown 8vo. ....*Cloth boards* 5 0

Church History in England,
From the Earliest Times to the Period of the Reforma-
tion. By the Rev. ARTHUR MARTINEAU, M.A. 12mo.
Cloth boards 3 0

s. d.

Church History, Sketches of,
From the first Century to the Reformation. By the Rev. J. C. ROBERTSON. With Map. 12mo...*Cloth boards* 2 0

Daily Readings for a Year.
By ELIZABETH SPOONER. Crown 8vo.......*Cloth boards* 3 6

Devotional (A) Life of our Lord.
By the Rev. E. L. CUTTS, D.D. Post 8vo. *Cloth boards* 5 0

Englishman's Brief, The,
On behalf of his National Church. New edition. Small post 8vo. .... *Paper boards* 0 6

Gospels, The Four,
Arranged in the Form of an English Harmony, from the Text of the Authorized Version. By the late Rev. J. M. FULLER, M.A. With Analytical Table of Contents and four Maps...*Cloth boards* 1 0

History of the English Church.
In short Biographical Sketches. By the Rev. JULIUS LLOYD, M.A., Author of "Sketches of Church History in Scotland." Post 8vo........................*Cloth boards* 1 6

History (A) of the Jewish Nation,
From the Earliest Times to the Present Day. By the late E. H. PALMER, M.A. With Map of Palestine and numerous Illustrations. Crown 8vo. ...... *Cloth boards* 4 '0

Lectures on the Historical and Dogmatical Position of the Church of England.
By the Rev. W. BAKER, D.D. Post 8vo....*Cloth boards* 1 6

Lesser Lights;
Or, some of the Minor Characters of Scripture traced, with a View to Instruction and Example in Daily Life. By the Rev. F. BOURDILLON, M.A. First and Second Series. Post 8vo......................*Cloth boards, each* 2 6
Third Series 2 0

On the Nature and Office of God the Holy Ghost.
By the Rev. S. C. AUSTEN, Vicar of Stokenchurch, Oxon. Fcap. 8vo. ....*Cloth boards* 1 0

s. d.

On the Origin of the Laws of Nature.
By Lord GRIMTHORPE. Post 8vo............*Cloth boards* 1 6

Paley's Evidences.
A New Edition, with Notes, Appendix, and Preface.
By the Rev. E. A. LITTON. Post 8vo.......*Cloth boards* 4 0

Paley's Horæ Paulinæ.
A New Edition, with Notes, Appendix, and Preface.
By the Rev. J. S. HOWSON, D.D., Dean of Chester.
Post 8vo. .... *Cloth boards* 3 0

Peace with God.
A Manual for the Sick. By the Rev. E. BURRIDGE, M.A.
Post 8vo. .... *Cloth boards* 1 6

Plain Reasons against Joining the Church of Rome.
By the Rev. R. F. LITTLEDALE, LL.D., &c. Revised
and enlarged edition. Post 8vo. .... *Cloth boards* 1 0

Plain Words for Christ.
Being a Series of Readings for Working Men. By the
late Rev. R. G. DUTTON, B.A. Post 8vo....*Cloth boards* 1 0

Prophecies and Types of Messiah.
Four Lectures to Pupil-Teachers. By the Rev. G. P.
OTTEY, M.A. Post 8vo........................*Cloth boards* 1 0

Religion for Every Day.
Lectures for Men. By the Right Rev. A. BARRY, D.D.
Fcap. 8vo. ....*Cloth boards* 1 0

Seek and Find.
A Double Series of Short Studies of the Benedicite. By
the late CHRISTINA G. ROSSETTI. Post 8vo. *Cloth boards* 2 6

Servants of Scripture, The.
By the late Rev. JOHN W. BURGON, B.D. Post 8vo.
Cloth boards 2 6

Some Chief Truths of Religion.
By the Rev. E. L. CUTTS, D.D., Author of " St. Cedd's
Cross," &c. Crown 8vo........................*Cloth boards* 2 6

s. d.

Story of the Church of England, A.
By Mrs. C. D. FRANCIS. Post 8vo. With twelve page
Illustrations ....*Cloth boards* 2 0

Thoughts for Men and Women.
The Lord's Prayer. By EMILY C. ORR. Post 8vo.
Limp cloth 1 0

Time Flies; a Reading Diary.
By the late CHRISTINA G. ROSSETTI. Post 8vo.
Cloth boards 2 6

True Vine, The.
By the late Mrs. RUNDLE CHARLES, Author of "The
Schönberg Cotta Family." Post 8vo. ......*Cloth boards* 1 6

Talks on Tithes. Why Pay them ?
By Farmers Hopgood, Cornfield, and Stockwell. Edited
by the Author of "The Englishman's Brief," &c. Post
8vo. ....*Paper covers* 0 6

Thoughts for Working Days.
Original and Selected. By EMILY C. ORR. Post 8vo.
Limp cloth 1 0

Turning-Points of English Church History.
By the Rev. E. L. CUTTS, D.D., Vicar of Holy Trinity,
Haverstock Hill. Crown 8vo. ....*Cloth boards* 3 6

Turning-Points of General Church History.
By the Rev. E. L. CUTTS, D.D., Author of "Pastoral
Counsels," &c. Crown 8vo. ....*Cloth boards* 4 0

Under His Banner.
Papers on Missionary Work of Modern Times. By the
Rev. W. H. TUCKER. Seventh Edition, with an Appendix
bringing the book up to 1897. With Map. Crown 8vo.
Half bound 5 0

LONDON : NORTHUMBERLAND AVENUE, W.C.;
43, QUEEN VICTORIA STREET, E.C.

BRIGHTON : 129, NORTH STREET.

www.ingramcontent.com/pod-product-compliance
Lightning Source LLC
Chambersburg PA
CBHW021529090426
42739CB00007B/846